T0149010

QUANTUM
OF SILLINESS

QUANTUM OF SILLINESS

THE PECULIAR WORLD OF BOND, JAMES BOND

ROBBIE SIMS

The
History
Press

For my BBF (Best Bond Friend) Dave;
and my very own Doctor Goodhead, Amir.

Cover artwork by Adrian Teal

First published 2020

The History Press
97 St George's Place, Cheltenham,
Gloucestershire, GL50 3QB
www.thehistorypress.co.uk

British Library Cataloguing in Publication Data.
A catalogue record for this book is available from the British Library.

ISBN 978 0 7509 9404 0

Typesetting and origination by The History Press
Printed and bound in Great Britain by TJ International Ltd.

ABOUT THE AUTHOR
OF ALL YOUR PAIN

When he was young and his heart was an open book, Robbie first fell under the spell of 007 while watching *Live and Let Die*. Consequently, he now finds himself checking the bathroom for snakes every time he shaves. He works as a scriptwriter and voice-over artist, and quite enjoys referring to himself in the third person. For the record: he thinks the best Bond film is *Casino Royale* (2006), the GREATEST Bond film is *The Spy Who Loved Me* (1977), and his personal favourite Bond film is *A View to a Kill* (1985) (which probably explains a lot). You can follow his daily Bondian dribblings on Twitter @TheTchaikovsky.

I've been looking FOREWORD to this moment, Mr Bond.

Do you really like James Bond? I do. I'm obsessed with the movies to the point that I spend my spare time pondering what a sequel to *Octopussy* might be called (*Eggpisode 2: Attack of the Clowns*?), or whether actress Honor Blackman should really consider changing her surname to Majesty's-SecretService. Oftentimes you'll find me lightly caressing the tattoo of Dame Judi Dench on my forehead (always a great conversation piece at job interviews – and there's been so many), whilst humming a few bars of John Barry's 'Dawn Raid on Fort Knox', then I'll perhaps channel my best Pola Ivanova and go sit in my Jacuzzi for a while to let the bubbles tickle my Tchaikovsky.

I feel the need for a disclaimer: this may not be the book for casual fans. If you don't know your Jinx from your Hinx, or can't differentiate between Monro (Matt) and Munro (Caroline), you risk being left more bewildered than an audience twenty minutes into *Quantum of Solace*.

So here's a quick test for you: which movie features a villain with an unconvincing dragon; and which movie features a villain with unconvincing drag on? If you've drawn a blank I'd recommend you bail at this point. I mean, thanks for reading thus far but frankly it's time you put this tome down and started re-evaluating your life choices. Only those with an in-depth (i.e. respectable) level of Bond knowledge will fully grasp what I'm on about across the following pages. (The answers, incidentally, are *Dr. No* and *Diamonds Are Forever* respectively.)

Still with me? In the words of Professor Joe Butcher: 'bless your heart'. Come with me as we explore who gives the hammiest performances of the franchise. We'll ponder what quips Sir Roger Moore would've come out with if he'd starred in *Licence to Kill*; and compile the appalling jokes *Diamonds Are Forever*'s Vegas comedian Shady Tree might have in his repertoire if he were performing to a room of Bond fans. We'll raid nefarious media baron Elliot Carver's Fake News files, we'll explore Q's haikus from his personal diary, and we'll undertake a much-needed dissection of just how spectacularly dodgy *Die Another Day* is. But most of all we'll be wallowing in ropey puns – enough ropey puns to make even the screenwriter of *Moonraker* blush.

So roll out the gunbarrel, pour yourself a vodka martini (dry) and climb into a sleek '70's submersible Lotus (wet) as we take an absurdist deep dive into the greatest movie franchise of them all. The weird and wonderful world of 007 is about to get a whole lot weirder … and negligibly more wonderful.

ALTERNATIVE TITLES FOR *DR. NO*

When Harry Met Cubby
Easy Ryder
The Trench Connection
How to Feign Your Dragon
Honey I Blew Up the Crab Key

SHADY TREE'S DODGY DAD JOKES ...

Q: What's Mr Big's favourite Britpop anthem?
A: Don't Look Back Kananga.

Q: What's the difference between a dim-witted cyborg policeman who battles the criminal schemes of Dr Claw, and James Bond's exploding Omega watch?
A: One's Inspector Gadget; the other's a gadget in *Spectre*.

Q: Which Bond songstress is handy to have nearby on a hot summer's day?
A: Rita Cool-fridge.

FROM ELLIOT CARVER'S FAKE NEWS FILES ...

Having supplied the screenplay for *You Only Live Twice*, Roald Dahl wrote a sequel – in which 007 has to sit through a two-hour evil masterplan monologue from Blofeld – called *James and the Giant Speech*.

© Rex Features

Q: What's Michelle Yeoh's favourite place to hang out in Jerusalem?
A: The Wai Lin Wall

BOND ACTORS WHOSE NAMES ARE ALSO INNUENDOES

Grand L. Bush
Honor Blackman
B.J. Worth
Roger Moore
Ursula … Undress?

THOUGHTS FROM
THE CUBBY HOLE...

Moore's final scene as 007 – necking in the shower with Stacey Sutton at the 'climax' of *A View to a Kill* – is begging for a direct-to-camera 'Roger and out'.

FOR BETTER OR FOR WORSE (BUT USUALLY WORSE) – INVITE 007 TO YOUR WEDDING AT YOUR PERIL …

You Only Live Twice: An arranged and somewhat deranged fake marriage helps Bond go undercover as a local Japanese villager. Imagine being the poor bride arriving at the top of that hill to find you're marrying a belligerent Scot who looks like he's into Vulcan cosplay.

On Her Majesty's Secret Service: Bond gets proper married! But a blubbing Miss Moneypenny and a boozed-up M bantering with his new crime-lord father-in-law are soon to be the least of 007's troubles … talk about a shotgun wedding.

Live and Let Die: Bond literally crashes the wedding by driving a speedboat right through a ceremony in Louisiana … a pursuer then unceremoniously drives right into the cake. What Q might call 'a gateau blaster'.

A View to a Kill: The cake is in tiers and the bride is in tears after RogBond's stunt double #142 literally drops in on this riverboat wedding party on the Seine.

Licence to Kill: Is Bond really the best man to play … a best man? He hijacks Felix and Della's big day for a bit of pre-titles tomfoolery, but at least he gets the groom to the church on time. Here's to 'a nice honeymoooon'.

ALTERNATIVE TITLES FOR
FROM RUSSIA WITH LOVE

Dial M For Murder On The Orient Express
Red Dead Redemption
(Kiss) My Left Foot
Hector the Spectre Defector about the Lektor
My Big Fat Gypsy Three-way

CLASSIC BOND QUOTES

James Bond: 'Do you mind if my friend sits this one out? She's somehow been shot across a crowded dancefloor and the bullet somehow went through my fingers and into her back and killed her instantly and somehow no one noticed. Cheers.' (*Thunderball*, 1965)

SPIN-OFF MOVIE PROPOSALS

Screwball comedy road trip with *Casino Royale*'s accident-prone poker players Infante and Gräfin Von Wallenstein, called *Ace in the Hole*.

Slapstick farce in which Francisco the Fearless is sacked from *Octopussy*'s circus and forced to find a job in the real world that somehow utilises his limited skillset as a human cannonball, called *Hire Me And/Or Fire Me*.

Gritty martial arts thriller in which *The Man With The Golden Gun*'s now adult and very vengeful river urchin tracks down 007 to collect his payment of 20,000 Baht, called *The Elephant Never Forgets*.

May Day's Dating Tip No.1: The racetrack is a great place to pick up men. (© Rex Features)

FROM ELLIOT CARVER'S FAKE NEWS FILES …

To bring authenticity to her role as Dr Christmas Jones, Denise Richards insisted upon spending several years studying nuclear physics at Yale University. She now works as a scantily clad cooling tower decontaminator at Sizewell B power station in Suffolk.

COMMISSION IMPOSSIBLE: BOND-THEMED REALITY TV PROPOSALS

Contestants try to out-act each other in the role of *Octopussy*'s demented General Orlov … *The Great British Berkoff*.

The fictional head of the KGB sits down with his assistant Rubelvitch to watch the week's television and relay his thoughts … *GogolBox*.

Blofeld's stocky Piz Gloria assistant eats kangaroo testes in the Australian outback … *Irma Celebrity Get Me Out Of Here!*

Fame-hungry narcissists shag each other in the Balearics, but only so they can get their hands on a Soviet Intelligence decoding machine … *From Russia With Love Island*.

Contestants compete to stop a Skyfleet airliner from being blown up at Miami International Airport … *Protect Runway*.

Competitors camp it up to see who can run fastest while dressed as a megalomaniac billionaire industrialist … *RuPaul's Drax Race.*

Trapped in a house 24/7 while cameras film their every move, contestants' resistance to heroin (and each other) is tested by a nefarious drug baron … *Mr Big Brother.*

Contestants open random boxes in an attempt to find which one hides a nymphomaniac ice skater called Bibi … *Dahl Or No Dahl.*

The Fabergé egg 'Property Of A Lady', modelled by proper hottie of a lady Maud Adams as Octopussy.

THOUGHTS FROM THE CUBBY HOLE...

If you're left traumatised after a particularly intense pre-title sequence, are you suffering from PTSPTSD?

ALTERNATIVE TITLES
FOR *GOLDFINGER*

Tilly Death Do Us Part
James Bond 3: Assignment Miami Beach
Frisky Galore!
Opportunity Knox
Solo: A Car Squash Story

YOU ONLY BOND TWICE: SOME UNORTHODOX 007 DOUBLE BILLS ...

The 'Shove A Woman In A Cupboard' Double Bill
(nb: this sort of behaviour is only acceptable if the cupboard-destined woman does so willingly, and preferably has a fetish for the smell of safari suits)

Live and Let Die: Having already 'de-briefed' Bond, Agent Caruso then gets to see how well hung his clothes are – bundled into his home wardrobe when M pays an unexpected visit.

The Man With The Golden Gun: Mary Goodnight becomes another closet case, flung into Bond's hotel wardrobe while he has his wicked way with Lady Scaramanga on the bed. Goodnight's sleep not guaranteed.

The 'Dump a Body in a Skip' Double Bill
(nb: this sort of behaviour is also never really acceptable, unless you're close to recycling day)

The World Is Not Enough: Davidov meets dumpster after being David-offed by Bond in Azerbaijan.

Quantum Of Solace: Mathis' corpse unceremoniously becomes La Paz Waste Disposal Authority's problem after he dies in Bond's arms.

The 'Tabasco' Double Bill
(hot condiment of choice for two Bond antagonists)

The Man With the Golden Gun: Scaramanga orders butler Nick Nack to fetch him a bottle in the opening scene.

The Spy Who Loved Me: Spotted on Stromberg's dining table, the saucy devil.

The 'Converse With a Rodent' Double Bill
(or: the pest of both worlds)

Diamonds Are Forever: Bond is placed in one of his EES (Easily Escapable Situations) – a newly constructed pipeline beneath the Nevada desert. Therein, he briefly enjoys a chat with a rat … 'One of us smells like a tart's handkerchief.'

Spectre: 'Who are you working for?' asks a bored Bond when he holds a Moroccan mouse at gunpoint in his L'Americain Hotel suite … Somehow one of the less wince-worthy interrogation scenes of the Craig era.

FROM ELLIOT CARVER'S
FAKE NEWS FILES …

Director Lewis Gilbert was such a fan of his leading lady in *The Spy Who Loved Me* that he collated all of the pictures of her in an extensive Bach catalogue.

ALTERNATIVE TITLES FOR *THUNDERBALL*

Nobody Does It Wetter
Never Say Nassau Again
Volpe Goes Bahamas
We Need To Talk About Kevin McClory
The Last Days of Disco Volante

SHADY TREE'S DODGY DAD JOKES ...

Q: Where do ski enthusiasts go when they can't afford a foreign holiday?
A: Willie Bognor Regis.

Q: What's the difference between Necros in *The Living Daylights* and Daniel Craig in *Casino Royale*?
A: One got the boot; the other got the reboot.

Q: What's the difference between Eminem and me?
A: One's The Real Slim Shady; the other's a real slimy Shady.

CLASSIC BOND QUOTES

James Bond arriving at Gustav Graves' Ice Palace: 'Does this place have a pool?'
Concierge: 'Only if we're attacked by a giant space laser sir.' (*Die Another Day*, 2002)

➔ Alizia Gur and Martine Beswick in a vicious catfight during *From Russia With Love*. They're rumoured to have been scrapping about which version of Dame Shirley Bassey's *Moonraker* is better – the ballad over the opening titles or the disco version at the end.
© Rex Features

SIR GODFREY TIBBETT'S TITBITS

A View to a Kill is the only Bond film in which the average age of the cast matches the year of its release (85).

THOUGHTS FROM THE CUBBY HOLE...

If you can't afford to download Eric Serra's *GoldenEye* score, simply gather some Gregorian chanters at the bottom of an aluminium stairwell and drop a pillowcase full of spanners on them.

Q'S HAIKUS (OR HAI-QS IF YOU'RE IN A HURRY)

Just met a James Bond
gave him my attaché case
seemed well up himself

Dispatched to Japan
not sure about Bond's new wig
looks kinda racist

In *Live and Let Die*
although my watch saves Bond loads
I wasn't cast. Sad.

Just made fake nipple
inside hull of *Queen Mary*
honestly, this job …

FROM ELLIOT CARVER'S FAKE NEWS FILES...

In a bid to remain central to the Bond zeitgeist in 1969, Honor Blackman considered changing her surname to Majesty's-Secretservice.

YOU ONLY LOOK TWICE – THE BONDVERSE'S BEST DOUBLE TAKES

Victor Tourjansky

All hail everyone's favourite dumbfounded boozehound Victor Tourjansky (credited as 'Man with Bottle' in *The Spy Who Loved Me* and *Moonraker,* and 'Man with Wine Glass' in *For Your Eyes Only*). This half-cut holidaymaker can't believe his eyes when 007 drives/skis/bondoliers past, and decides to blame the bottle.

Incidentally, since he's popped up in Italy three times already, wouldn't it be the perfect piece of EON fan service if Victor made a cameo during *No Time to Die*'s DB5 action sequence? Stick him in Matera Town Square with a bottle of Lambrusco, you cowards.

Venetian Pigeon, *Moonraker*

Much maligned by audiences at the time, but now well beloved (very much the avian antithesis to Kevin Spacey in this regard), is there a more iconic bird in all of cinema? Aside from *For Your Eyes Only*'s Max the Parrot obviously.

Sir Roger Moore, All The Time

No-one doubles down on the double take quite like Rodge. So many great examples across his 007 tenure to choose from. Notable examples include realising he's being held at gunpoint by Anya at the end of *The Spy Who Loved Me*, and seeing Melina's 2CV getaway vehicle for the first time in *For Your Eyes Only*.

Timothy Dalton, *Licence to Kill*

Who'd have thought with an increasingly swivel-eyed Roger hamming his way through seven adventures, it would be ThespBond himself T-Dalt who delivers the most pronounced double take of the franchise? When a freshly spruced Pam Bouvier arrives at Banco de Isthmus she makes heads turn – most notably 007's, who practically dislocates his neck in the process.

ALTERNATIVE TITLES FOR
YOU ONLY LIVE TWICE

Mr Kiss Kissy Bang Bang
Drag Me To Helga
Attack of the Killer Osato
James Versus the Volcano
The First (in Oriental Languages) and the Furious:
Tokyo Drift

Licence to Kill spin-off movie proposal: *Dirty Sanchez* with the tagline 'With Franz like this, who needs enemies?'

CLASSIC BOND QUOTES

Max Zorin: 'Intuitive improvisation is the secret of genius, it says here in my script.' (*A View to a Kill*, 1985)

SPIN-OFF MOVIE PROPOSALS

Heist caper which repositions *From Russia With Love*'s Aryan *Spectre* assassin as a lovable rogue who raids the vaults of Europe's biggest casinos, called *Always Bet On Red*.

Supernatural origins story for *Live and Let Die*'s Solitaire, entitled *Cards On The Table*.

Vividly coloured pre-school animation featuring the adventures of *Live and Let Die*'s Louisiana State Sheriff, called *Pepper Pig*.

SHADY TREE'S DODGY DAD JOKES ...

Q: What's Dr Carl Mortner's preferred cinema projection format?
A: 'IMAAAAAX!'

Q: Why does the head of Osato Chemicals & Engineering find Milton Krest's death scene from *Licence to Kill* so distressing?
A: Because 'Mr Osato believes in a healthy Krest'.

Q: What's the difference between *No Time to Die*'s script development and *A View to a Kill*?
A: One culminates with Phoebe Waller-Bridge and one culminates with falling off a bridge.

ALTERNATIVE TITLES FOR *ON HER MAJESTY'S SECRET SERVICE*

My Big Fat Bleak Wedding
A View To A Kilt
A Matter Of Wife And Death
War & Piz
James and the Giant Piste

THUNDERBRAWL – FANTASY FISTICUFFS BETWEEN DISPARATE BOND CHARACTERS …

Hans (*You Only Live Twice*) versus **Necros** (*The Living Daylights*) in a battle of the generic Aryan henchmen. Necros prevails with his garrotting Walkman, and for looking the hottest in Speedos.

Auric Goldfinger versus **Corrine Dufour** (*Moonraker*) in a battle of the most-gratuitously over-dubbed character. Goldfinger triumphs after Corinne hotfoots it through the woods in her wellingtons while someone in a dubbing studio does all the panting/screaming.

Plenty O'Toole (*Diamonds Are Forever*) versus **Penelope Smallbone** (*Octopussy*) in a battle of the women whose names allude to penis size. Unsurprisingly, Plenty comes first.

Andrea Anders (*The Man With The Golden Gun*) versus **Octopussy** (*checks notes* *Octopussy*) in a battle to see who can do the best Maud Adams impression. Octopussy wins simply for having a really awesome personalized dressing gown/bed/banister.

Oddjob (*Goldfinger*) versus **Gobinda** (*Octopussy*) in a battle of the henchmen who crush sporting accessories into dust with their bare hands (golf balls and dice respectively). Oddjob wins by default when adjudicators rule that backgammon isn't really a sport.

Sheriff J.W. Pepper (*Live and Let Die* & *The Man With The Golden Gun*) versus **Jack Wade** (*GoldenEye* and *Tomorrow Never Dies*) in a smackdown of lazy American stereotypes who appear in a Bond actor's first two consecutive adventures. Pepper wins by overpowering his opponent with sheer levels of obnoxiousness.

Jaws (*The Spy Who Loved Me* & *Moonraker*) versus **Bullion** (*The World Is Not Enough*) in a clash of the metal-mouthed muscle. Jaws wins because he's freakin' Jaws, and what the hell did Bullion ever do except leg it from an exploding suitcase?

Sharon (Q Branch assistant in *For Your Eyes Only*) versus **Karen** (Q Branch assistant in *Octopussy*). The gadget-testing subordinates grapple for supremacy before deciding to join forces and smash their way to freedom through MI6's patriarchal glass ceiling. Match postponed.

A BOND VILLAIN LIMERICK

There once was a Dr Kananga,
Prone to bouts of great anger.
He'd shout down the place,
And pull of his face …
Dude needs to chill like Scaramanga.

Roger Moore and Barbara Bach were keen advocates of yoga every day while on set at Pinewood. Here they can be seen adopting the Lotus position.

FROM ELLIOT CARVER'S
FAKE NEWS FILES …

Timothy Dalton was so convincing as a pretend manta ray in *Licence to Kill* he was later asked to reprise the role for James Cameron's *The Abyss*. He also played a jellyfish in an episode of Baywatch but the scene was cut to accommodate more slow-motion breasts.

CLASSIC BOND QUOTES

Scaramanga: 'He ain't Herve, he's my butler.' (*The Man With The Golden Gun*, 1974)

SHADY TREE'S DODGY DAD JOKES ...

Q: Which Bond actress loves incubating and birthing Easter chicks?
A: Teri HATCHER.

Q: Did you know Christoph Waltz once wrote a book about French bread?
A: He's the author of *All Your Pain*.

Q: What's the (admittedly not only) difference between *For Your Eyes Only* and *Moonraker*?
A: One involves keelhauling and the other involves (Richard) Kiel falling (out of a plane).

In *Skyfall* Bond realises there's a piece of London he hasn't blown up yet and quickly rushes to the scene. (© Rex Features)

THOUGHTS FROM THE CUBBY HOLE...

Prince Charles gave *No Time to Die* some early publicity when he toured the set at Pinewood Studios in June 2019. To be honest, I'm surprised he's even on speaking terms with EON after they made his mum sit through 2002's royal premiere of *Die Another Day*.

BINGE ON CRINGE

Take a breath and count to ten; these are the Bond moments most likely to have you squirming in your chair faster than a visit from Le Chiffre with a knotted rope …

Dr. No

It's somehow an understood rule within the Bond universe that 007 will always be the alpha male in any given circumstance – a sort of default Bond Supremacy (see how he takes command of a deferent Columbo's cronies, who he's never previously met, during the Albania dock raid in *For Your Eyes Only*) – but that really doesn't excuse his treatment of local hired help Quarrel on the beach at Crab Key, whom he brusquely orders to 'Fetch my shoes'. It's the sort of cringeworthy colonialism that permeated much of Ian Fleming's work. Jamaica would gain independence from the British Empire only a few months before the movie was released.

Goldfinger

All art is a product of its time and should be regarded accordingly. Nevertheless, having Bond force himself on a self-declared lesbian until she 'turns straight' doesn't look great now and can't have looked that heroic in 1964. Less sensual, more non-consensual: rarely has a roll in the hay seemed more retrograde.

You Only Live Twice
Is he turning Japanese? I think he's turning Japanese; I really think so. Sadly 007's ethnicity realignment surgery – an attempt to go undercover as a local fisherman – results in something more akin to Mr Spock Star Trek cosplay. There's no disguising the awkwardness of this maladroit makeover.

On Her Majesty's Secret Service
The best way to subdue a hysterical woman during a daring mountaintop raid? Knock her unconscious and bundle her into a helicopter. A hard slap from Daddy Draco should do it. Ouch indeed.

The Man With The Golden Gun
Sir Roger Moore would later state, from his perspective as Goodwill Ambassador for U.N.I.C.E.F, that this was his most regrettable moment portraying Bond: pushing a young urchin into a Bangkok canal after said child has literally just helped save 007's life. Still, no ill feelings – aside from suspected typhoid?

Octopussy
RogBond's clown get-up is often cited as a nadir of the franchise, but actually the disguise is a necessary one and the bomb defusing sequence is made all

the more tense because of it. The film's insistence to acknowledge every lazy Indian stereotype under the post-colonial sun is discomforting in a less intended way (a random market square scene somehow includes a sword swallower, a fakir on a bed of nails and gurus walking on hot coals), as is the line 'that'll keep you in curry for a while'. Dishonourable mention for that Tarzan yell too.

A View to a Kill
Much like a snowboarding Bond in this pre-titles sequence, things go downhill rapidly when John Barry's rousing score lurches clumsily into 'California Girls' by The Beach Boys (as performed here by Gidea Park). God only knows how this made it to the final cut.

The Living Daylights
In deepest Afghanistan, Bond finds himself joining forces with Osama Bin Laden's old muckers the Mujahideen ... Time has not treated this plot development well: these anti-Russian jihadist freedom fighters might have suited 1987's Cold War sensibilities, but 007 basically teams up with the Taliban.

Die Another Day
Where to start? Whitewashed villains, ice palaces, tsunami surfing, pretty much every line of dialogue Jinx has to spout – this whole movie is more toe-curling than a visit to an over-enthusiastic foot masseur.

Spectre

Spoiler alert: Blofeld is Bond's step-brother who bears a life-long grudge against 007 because ... daddy didn't love him as much as he loved James! A cringeworthy plot lifted straight from a Bond spoof movie (Dr Evil and Austin Powers are revealed as long-lost brothers in *Goldmember*, released thirteen years prior), this has the unique honour of not only making Bond24 a hot mess, it retroactively renders the plots of Daniel Craig's previous three Bond movies really quite nonsensical too.

ALTERNATIVE TITLES FOR
DIAMONDS ARE FOREVER

Break Franks At Tiffany's
Good Willard Hunting
Horn of Plenty
Honey, I Blew Up Mr Kidd
Mobsters Inc

FROM ELLIOT CARVER'S FAKE NEWS FILES...

Before arriving at 'Strawberry Fields', several other Beatles references were considered for the name of *Quantum of Solace*'s oil-fated Bond woman. These included: Eleanor Rigby, Penny Lane, Abi Road and Kate Daysaweek.

THOUGHTS FROM THE CUBBY HOLE …

It's almost impossible to not be in the mood to watch the first 75% of *Tomorrow Never Dies*.

'BUT OF COURSE YOU ARE …'

How literal are Bond actors' names?

Jane Seymour: Does see more, yes (into the future as clairvoyant Solitaire).

Roger Moore: Does indeed roger more (as Bond he bedded more women than any other actor).

Christoph Waltz: Can't even be bothered to foxtrot.

Christopher Walken: Yes, when he's not riding (he's happiest … in the saddle).

Alan Cumming: No ejaculations witnessed on screen, thankfully.

Rik Van Nutter: Never seen enthusing about any kind of large road vehicle.

Carole Bouquet: Seen outside a flower shop as Melina in Italy, I guess.

The World Is Not Enough spin-off movie proposal: *I'm Dreaming Of A Wet Christmas,* with the tagline: We'll make you weak at Denise. (© Rex Features)

ALTERNATIVE TITLES FOR
LIVE AND LET DIE

Dicks of Hazzard
Look Back Kananga
Stop! Or My Coconut Will Shoot
Planes Trains and Pimpmobiles
Snake's On A Plain White Rug

FROM ELLIOT CARVER'S
FAKE NEWS FILES …

On the set of *The Man With The Golden Gun*, Bernard Lee and Christopher Lee held a duel to see who was the Ultimate Lee. It would be ungentlemanly to reveal the victor, but let's just say Bernard refused to leave his suite at the Hong Kong Radisson for the remainder of filming.

YOU ONLY BOND TWICE – SOME MORE UNORTHODOX 007 DOUBLE BILLS …

The 'Butterflies' Double Bill
(Wings, but not the Paul McCartney kind)

On Her Majesty's Secret Service: 007 discovers M is a keen lepidopterist during a visit to his country home … these are not the kind of bugs Bond is used to dealing with.
A View to a Kill: Dominique – simply credited as 'whistling girl' – conducts a frankly bewildering performance with a swarm of fake butterflies at the Eiffel Tower's restaurant, yet still manages to be the most plausible part of this legendarily daft scene.

The 'Someone Locked in a Boot' Double Bill
('They got the Boot!')

The Man With The Golden Gun: The mishap-prone Mary Goodnight finds herself trunk-ated inside

Scaramanga's flying AMC Matador coupé.
Quantum Of Solace: Two boot lock-ins for the price of one here, with Mr White shoved in Bond's rear end in the pre-titles, while a worse for wear Mathis later finds himself unwitting stowaway in the back of Bond's Range Rover.

The 'Mutilated Earlobe' Double Bill
(They don't expect you to talk and you shouldn't expect them to listen … these villains aren't quite 'all ears')

On Her Majesty's Secret Service: Blofeld lops his lobes off in a bid to claim the aristocratic title 'Comte Balthazar de Bleuchamp', but you can call him Ernie.
The World Is Not Enough: Elektra hacks off her own left ear-dangle so kidnapper Renard can send it to her father as a warning (not to get her earrings for her birthday, presumably).

Incidentally, that's not the only random connection between these two movies … both feature Bond getting buried by snow, Bond references the Caspian Sea in both (and both feature caviar), both reference Christmas, both pre-titles are set in London and Iberia, and of course both reference Bond's family motto. Glad I got that out of my system.

CLASSIC BOND QUOTES

Rosa Klebb punching Red Grant in the abs: 'He seems fit enough, except for his spleen, which I just ruptured with my knuckleduster, testing if he was fit enough. Have him report to me in Istanbul in 24 hours.' (*From Russia With Love*, 1963)

FIVE PLEASING JAMES BOND COINCIDENCES …

🔫 Lazenby's Bond literally gets down on one knee in his gunbarrel sequence, then figuratively gets down on one knee to propose to Tracy.

🔫 In *The Spy Who Loved Me*, when the RAF helicopter pilot says 'Roger out' it's immediately followed by Roger getting out.

🔫 Bedding Roger twice (in *The Man With The Golden Gun* and then *Octopussy*) means that as a Bond girl, Maud Adams is a more Moored Adams.

🔫 At the climax of *A View to a Kill* we see RogBond aptly hanging from a 'mooring' rope on the front of Zorin's blimp.

🔫 Pierce Brosnan's *Die Another Day* bod is an actual DAD bod.

ALTERNATIVE TITLES FOR *THE MAN WITH THE GOLDEN GUN*

Honey I Shrunk The Henchman
Mr Kiss Kiss Bangkok
Solex and Violence
The Talented Mr Triply-Nipple
Goodnight and Phu Yuck

FROM ELLIOT CARVER'S
FAKE NEWS FILES …

Having supplied the Aston Martin DB5, the V8 Vantage, the DBS Superleggera and the Valhalla to the set of *No Time to Die*, the iconic car company are now looking ahead to Bond's twenty-sixth movie and developing a vehicle/director hybrid that's really skilled at introducing audiences to a new 007, called the Aston Martin Campbell.

SHOCKING, POSITIVELY SHOCKING: A CELEBRATION OF *DIE ANOTHER DAY'S* DIRE WAYS

James Bond movies have always existed in their own hyper-fantastical world ... but here's double-oh-seven times EON's twentieth movie kidnaps the very concept of logic and skis it off a cliff without so much as a union flag parachute ...

☞ After being rescued from his fourteen-month Korean torture ordeal, Bond escapes from hospital by slowing his heart rate down to the extent that his cardiogram flatlines. (Scientists will tell you that this is a medical impossibility, but admittedly anyone watching *Thunderball*'s turgid underwater sequences can achieve similar results.)

☞ In the same scene, Bond uses the hospital's defibrillator to shock and stun the two doctors who rush to his bedside, which apart from being physically impossible (defibrillator paddles don't work individually) seems the height of ingratitude.

☛We encounter Zao in a private clinic in Cuba. He's undergoing 'DNA restructuring' to make him look Caucasian (let's gloss over the impossibility and tone-deafness of all that) but … he still has diamonds embedded in his face from the pre-titles. So is the clinic going to restructure the DNA of the diamonds too? Come now Zao, even I know to remove my nipple piercings before undergoing a CT scan (that my doctors advised after hearing I've repeatedly watched this brain-dead movie).

☛Okay … the invisible car. Everyone loves to dump on DAD's Aston Martin 'Vanish' but the concept was at least based on military tech being developed at the time. I don't find this much-maligned gadget any more bonkers than, say, a submersible Lotus or a magnetic watch that can alter the path of a bullet. Yet there's a short scene with the car in Iceland where it's logic itself that totally disappears. As Cleese-Q himself states, the invisible car works thanks to adaptive camouflage – tiny cameras project the image they see onto a light-emitting polymer skin on the other side … So why does Bond hide from Graves' security guards behind the car when in invisible mode? His hunkered form would be broadcast on the other side of the Aston for everyone to see! Talk about hiding in plain sight.

☞There's a henchman called Mr Kil. Not beyond the realms of possibility admittedly, but considering Bond's fine tradition of single entendre character names, we're really scraping the bottom of the gunbarrel with this guy.

☞Melting ice palaces that somehow don't melt in a way to allow Jinx to escape, an ergonomic robo-suit rustled up in next to no time, M deciding to visit Korea's DMZ just as it's being fried from beyond the stratosphere … The final act of *Die Another Day* is a final act of defiance against any semblance of common sense. Of particular note is the plane full of jet engine fuel flying through the beam of a space laser and somehow not spontaneously combusting.

☞The film is at a climax and so is Moneypenny. As Sam Bond pulls BrosBond in for a snog that's been twenty movies in the making, it's revealed that she's simply acting out her fantasy in Q's VR machine. Which is all well and good but exactly who programmed a government-owned simulator to become Moneypenny's own stimulator? Sigmund Freud: analyse that.

THOUGHTS FROM THE CUBBY HOLE …

'I'm not interested in your sordid escapades,' says Q to Bond in *Tomorrow Never Dies* … the same man who once piloted his surveillance snooper dog into a stranger's house to watch 007 hump a lady in the shower.

ALTERNATIVE TITLES FOR THE SPY WHO LOVED ME

Get Commander Carter
The Partially Iron Giant
Mandible of Steel
Mrs Ringo Starr Wars: Anya Hope
Derek Meddings, Sandor Funeral

The ceremonial planting of Timothy Dalton back in 1989 was deemed such a success, it's now an annual event at Pinewood. Dalton traditionally remains in situ for several weeks absorbing essential nutrients from the Buckinghamshire soil.

MORE OF Q'S HAIKUS

Saw Bond shag Goodhead
made quip about re-entry
quite pleased with myself

Just flew a balloon
to Octopussy's palace
need more viagra

Made a new gadget
it's called a ghetto blaster
(check if offensive)

Bond wrote off my boat
chasing some bird down the Thames
can't wait to retire

FROM ELLIOT CARVER'S
FAKE NEWS FILES …

Diana Rigg was such a fan of Pierce Brosnan's final Bond movie that she considered changing her surname to Verday.

ALTERNATIVE TITLES FOR *MOONRAKER*

May The Farce Be With You
1979: A Space Oddity
Jaws 2: We're Gonna Need A Bigger Budget
Close Encounters of the Absurd Kind
Shuttle-Cocked: The Holly Goodhead Story

OVERCOOKED ACTING CHOPS

Celebrating The Bondverse's Hammiest Performances...

Steven Berkoff as General Orlov (*Octopussy*): 'The West is decadent' and so is Berkoff's magnificently bonkers performance. Never has the pronunciation of 'Czechoslovakia' been delivered with more zest.

Jean Rougerie as Mr Aubergine (*A View to a Kill*): How French is too French? This guy channels Hercule Poirot, René from *'Allo 'Allo* and every lazy Gallic stereotype going into a performance cheesier than a croissant crammed with Camembert. NB: despite having a very French-sounding name, I'm pretty sure no genuine French person was ever called Aubergine.

Lucien Jérôme as French taxi driver (*A View to a Kill*): Another baffling Parisian portrayal follows hot on the hor-he-hor-heels of Mr Aubergine. Bond commandeers a taxi driver's Renault ... the driver is drinking red wine out of a plastic cup (standard authentic local behaviour), then exclaims 'oh ma caaarrrr!' in English but with a thick French accent, as all proud residents of La République are want to do.

Clifton James as Sheriff J.W. Pepper (*Live and Let Die and The Man With The Golden Gun*): OTT for sure, but chewing tobacco together with scenery is exactly what the role of a redneck policeman demands. Prime slices of hammery from this racist pig.

Robert Rietty as voice of 'Blofeld' (*For Your Eyes Only*): Ham with added cackling. The glorious voice-only performance from Rietty in this not-official-but-very-obviously-Blofeld cameo relishes every appalling pun ('I hope you have a pleasant … fright!') and weirdly poetic non sequitur ('We can do a deal! I'll buy you a delicatessen in stainless steel!').

Uncredited extra as Chinese Army Officer (*Diamonds Are Forever*): A red star is born … This dude gets approximately two seconds of screen time but boy does he sell his role. One moment he's chilling by some communist military equipment; the next he's having his brain fried by Blofeld's diamond-encrusted space laser, and he's not afraid to show it.

Toby Stephens as Gustav Graves (*Die Another Day*): Someone contact Pinewood's authorities because Toby's sneering villain is stealing every scene he's in. All credit to Stephens, cranking up the ham is exactly what this pantomime role requires.

Veruschka von Lehndorff as Gräfin von Wallenstein (*Casino Royale*): Despite having zero lines of dialogue, this camp vamp of a poker player speaks volumes with her shoulder pads and soul-piercing glares. Veruschka's the extra giving it that little bit extra.

Jonathan Pryce as Elliot Carver (*Tomorrow Never Dies*): Overstated and underrated: we haven't witnessed a Bond villain chew the scenery like this since Jaws … and he did it literally.

Javier Bardem as Raoul Silva (*Skyfall*): Further proof that perfect Bond villainy often means dialling the swivel-eyed nuttiness up to eleven. No surprise that Javier also starred in Spanish comedy-drama Jamón Jamón … this is the hammiest performance since *Babe 2: Pig in the City*.

FROM ELLIOT CARVER'S FAKE NEWS FILES

Some folk say the oft amazing Christoph Waltz was wasted as Blofeld, but in fact the actor shot most of his scenes in the mornings and would only get properly wasted after midday.

ALTERNATIVE TITLES FOR
FOR YOUR EYES ONLY

Property of an Iron Lady
Panic A.T.A.C.
Victor Tourjansky 3: Still Drunk, Still Dumbfounded
Man of Stainless Steel
The Last Temptation of Kristatos

SHADY TREE'S DODGY DAD JOKES

Q: Why was *GoldenEye*'s villain only ever popular on dress-down Fridays?
A: Because no one likes a smart Alec.

Q: Why did *Live and Let Die*'s Tee Hee approach *The Living Daylight*'s Brad Whitaker when looking for a weaponised prosthetic limb?
A: Because Brad's an arms dealer.

Q: What's the difference between *For Your Eyes Only*'s title sequence and *You Only Live Twice*?
A: One involves Sheena Easton and the other involves Sean (Far Eastern).

A BOND VILLAIN LIMERICK

There once was a man called Drax,
Partial to inhumane acts.
He went off into space,
To start a super-race,
After causing global nerve gas attacks.

'WE CAN DO A DEAL!' FIVE BONDIAN BUSINESS IDEAS

☞007 fast food café called **No Time to Diet.**

☞ *Thunderball*-themed nightclub called **Disco Volante.**

☞*Tomorrow Never Dies/You Only Live Twice* fusion-theme restaurant called **Michelle Yeoh Sushi.**

☞A shop that just sells those little plastic bits at the end of laces called **Quantum Of Shoelace.**

☞A milliner that specializes in re-enforcing the brims of hats with metal called **Oddjob's Rimjobs.**

Misunderstanding his orders to go undercover to
infiltrate a volcano, Bond is made over as a Vulcan in
You Only Live Twice.

FROM ELLIOT CARVER'S FAKE NEWS FILES ...

Most believe he's a neat callback to *Dr. No*'s Bond ally Quarrel, but the character of Quarrel Jr is actually so-called because actor Roy Stewart could often be heard arguing with Harry Saltzman about who had fathered the most illegitimate children.

ALTERNATIVE TITLES
FOR *OCTOPUSSY*

Maud Adams 2: Armed & Fabulous
East Is East (Buckinghamshire)
Proper Hotty of a Lady
From Russia With Orlov
Never Say Never Say Never Again Again

NO TIME TO DIALOGUE

Do you expect them to talk?! For these henchmen, action speaks louder than words …

Oddjob: If silence is golden, it's no wonder Auric Goldfinger took a shine to this monosyllabic muscleman whose only vocal ejaculations start and end with 'UH!'

Hans: Lacking in loquacity, Blofeld's burly bodyguard in *You Only Live Twice* is further proof that every evil genius needs a dumb dogsbody.

Whisper: Compared to these other henchfellows, *Live and Let Die*'s Whisper speaks volumes … but only the volumes indiscernible to the human ear.

Jaws: The definitive strong but silent type. Ol' metalmouth is no motormouth, although dialogue with Dolly means he's practically got verbal diarrhoea by the end of *Moonraker*, uttering four words: 'Well, here's to us.'

Chang: Although partial to a kendo attack-scream in *Moonraker*, words mostly escape him – as does Bond … repeatedly.

Locque: Further proof that a lot of hitmen are much like the best farts: silent but deadly. This one from *For Your Eyes Only* is more tight-lipped than his identigraph mugshot might suggest.

Mollaka: Making bombs for a mysterious organization and jumping about miraculously across a construction site? He's your man. Making mouth-sounds as a means of rudimentary communication? Forget it … his 'ellipsis' are sealed.

Carlos Nikolic: While running amok at Miami International, another of *Casino Royale*'s taciturn terrorists literally has nothing to declare.

Patrice: Utterly utterless in *Skyfall*, Silva's hard-drive-snaffling minion seemingly prefers railways coaches to vocal coaches.

Mr Hinx: The critical response to *Spectre* may have been muted … but then so was its henchman.

FROM ELLIOT CARVER'S FAKE NEWS FILES...

Kylie Minogue's single 'All The Lovers' is a smash hit electro-pop ode to Bond's loaded deck of tarot cards in *Live and Let Die*.

ALTERNATIVE TITLES FOR
NEVER SAY NEVER AGAIN

You Only Leave Twice
Only Falls and Horses
Maximillian Ways to Die in the West (Indies)
It'll All End in Tears of Allah
Mad Maximillian: Beyond Thunderball

SIR GODFREY TIBBETT'S TITBITS

When casting EON's first Bond film, Ian Fleming's Jamaica neighbour Noel Coward was considered for the part of Dr No, until cinematographer Ted Moore pointed out he was simply too smug.

Whereas *Licence to Kill*'s poster proclaimed that Dalton-Bond's bad side was a dangerous place to be, it seems Connery's bad side was a dungarees place to be.

THOUGHTS FROM THE CUBBY HOLE …

If you laid all the abysmal scenes from *Die Another Day* end to end, you're probably the movie's editor.

ALTERNATIVE TITLES FOR
A VIEW TO A KILL

Moore! Moore Power!
Mr Kiss Kiss San Fran
Dude, Where's 'Ma Caaarr'?
James and the Giant Quiche
Dead Man Walken

CLASSIC BOND QUOTES

Concierge: 'Would you like to order anything from our room service menu, sir?'
James Bond: 'No thanks, I've already Eaton."
(*Goldfinger*, 1964)

SPIN-OFF MOVIE PROPOSALS

A remake of *The Spy Who Loved Me,* but from the perspective of henchman Jaws, called *The Spy Who Loathed Me.*

A remake of *You Only Live Twice,* but from the perspective of the Japanese Secret Service's Tiger Tanaka, called *Crouching Tiger Hidden Volcano Lair.*

Slice-of-life kitchen sink drama starring *Tomorrow Never Dies'* Teutonic pistol marksman Dr Kaufmann, entitled *Just Another Germanic Gun Day.*

FROM ELLIOT CARVER'S FAKE NEWS FILES ...

With Jeffrey Wright returning to play Bond's CIA friend for a third time in *No Time to Die*, producers considered renaming his character Threelix Leiter.

Re: promotion for *The Man With The Golden Gun*: in terms of gravitas, Roger Moore and Christopher Lee did most of the heavy lifting. In terms of gravity, Britt Ekland and Maud Adams did most of the Herve lifting.

IF BOND MOVIES WERE NAMED LIKE CARRY ON FILMS

Dr No  Carry On Doctor (No)

From Russia With Love Carry On Spying

Goldfinger Carry Honor Blackman

Thunderball Carry On Underwater

You Only Live Twice Carry On Mr Fisher

On Her Majesty's Secret Service Carry On Downhill Rapidly

Diamonds Are Forever Carry On Connerying

Live and Let Die Carry On Up The Bayou

The Man With The Golden Gun Carry On Sheriff

The Spy Who Loved Me Carry On Cubby

Moonraker Carry On Camping It Up

For Your Eyes Only 🔫 Carry On Columbo

Octopussy 🔫 Carry On Follow That Kamal

A View to a Kill 🔫 Carry On Rogering Moore

The Living Daylights 🔫 Carry On Don't Lose Your Head Of Section V

Licence to Kill 🔫 Carey Lowell

Goldeneye 🔫 Carry Onatopp

Tomorrow Never Dies 🔫 Carry On Up The Carver

The World is Not Enough 🔫 It's A Very Carry On Christmas

Die Another Day 🔫 Carry On Regardless Of Credibility

Casino Royale 🔫 Carry On Campbell

Quantum Of Solace 🔫 Carry On Where The Last One Left Off

Skyfall 🔫 Carry On Disrespecting The Gunbarrel Sequence

Spectre 🔫 Carry On Going Rogue. Every. Single. Film.

No Time to Die 🔫 Cary On Directing Duties

ALTERNATIVE TITLES FOR
THE LIVING DAYLIGHTS

Breaking Brad
Much Ad'abo About Nothing
Gibraltared States
Pushkin Daisies (he should've brought lilies)
Orchestral Manoeuvres in the Snow

FROM ELLIOT CARVER'S FAKE NEWS FILES

Sean Connery and Lois Maxwell were once conjoined twins. This rare archive picture was taken just prior to their separative operation funded by Sean's Mr Universe winnings (forced to tag along, Lois would hide under a blanket on stage during the famed muscle and oil fest).

THOUGHTS FROM THE CUBBY HOLE...

My favourite moment in *Skyfall*? Probably when Albert Finney takes Dame Judi up the priest hole.

NEW Q'S HAIKUS

Silva has hacked us
surprised I still have a job…
o.m.g. M's dead!

James nicked new Aston,
off to Austria to help
who will feed my cats?

CLASSIC BOND QUOTES

James Bond: 'There's always the hope that this underwater sequence might end soon but – counter-intuitively – I wouldn't hold your breath.' (*Thunderball*, 1965)

ALTERNATIVE TITLES FOR
LICENCE TO KILL

Dirty Sanchez
Mister Kiss Kiss Bang Pam
Rogue One: A John Glen Story
My Krest Friend's Beheading
May Felix's Best Man Win

CLASSIC BOND QUOTES

Chew Mee: 'Hi, I'm Chew Mee. I serve no real narrative purpose, but have you checked out my saucy name and my underwater muff? Byeeee!' (*The Man With The Golden Gun*, 1974)

PUTTING THE 'FUN' INTO THE FUNEREAL

007 may have No Time to Die, but plenty others did …

Dr. No: In what's arguably Bond's first cinematic action sequence, things go downhill rapidly for the hearse carrying the Three Blind Mice assassins. 'I think they were on their way to a funeral,' jests our hero.

Thunderball: 'The dead are alive' thanks to Jacques Bouvar … Spectre number 6 quickly finds his fake funeral to be a self-fulfilling prophecy. Well, at least he's already got a made-to-order coffin sorted.

You Only Live Twice: When it comes to the ladies he's always partial to some navel action, but here 007 enjoys some naval action. Another fake funeral, this time involving Bond's military burial at sea. 'Just a drop in the ocean,' as 007 later quips.

Diamonds Are Forever: Bond has a 'coffin' fit when nearly cremated at Slumber Inc.'s funeral parlour. Sorry for your loss (of interest during the latter stages of this film).

Live and Let Die: Funerals, gravestones, coffins, an actual character who may be undead? Morbid fascination runs riot in Bond's seventh adventure. Good grief indeed.

Moonraker: Gondola Roger turns coffin-dodger when a 'corpse' rises from his water-cortege casket and starts chucking knives at him – remarkably it's one of the least ludicrous moments from the Venice sequence.

For Your Eyes Only: Okay, not a funeral as such, but Bond is seen paying his respects at his late wife's grave in the pre-titles. It looks like a charming English graveyard, but then I've always maintained this movie has a great plot.

Spectre: How soon is too soon? Bond seduces a widow at the wake of her own husband's funeral – which he caused! Clearly death becomes her as she's barely finished burying the old man before she's burying her face in Bond's chest. Well, I guess she's not a mourning person.

FROM ELLIOT CARVER'S
FAKE NEWS FILES

Formerly obese actor Rik Van Nutter lost nearly 70 per cent of his body weight after misunderstanding an answerphone message from his agent that said, 'the producers of *Thunderball* want you to be Leiter'.

ALTERNATIVE TITLES
FOR *GOLDENEYE*

Joe Don Baker 2: Joe Don Bakerer
Ice Cold In Alec's (liquid nitrogen)
006 Days, Severnaya Nights
Calamity Janus
The Explodingpendables

THOUGHTS FROM THE CUBBY HOLE …

The holding company responsible for the copyright and trademarks to the characters, elements, and other material related to James Bond on screen is called DANJAQ … a combination of Broccoli and Saltzman's respective wives' names (**DAN**a Broccoli and **JA**c**Q**ueline Saltzman). So it's just as well they didn't marry women called Wanda and Kerry.

SHADY TREE'S DODGY DAD JOKES

Q: What's the difference between *Tomorrow Never Dies'* Wai Lin and Herr Stamper?
A: One's working undercover; the other's working under Carver.

Q: Did you hear about the version of *The Spy Who Loved Me* that doesn't feature the character M?
A: It's called *The Spy Who Loved E* and sees Bond whizzing his tits off to the Chemical Brothers in the back seat of a Lotus Esprit.

Q: Why did Daniel Craig ignore the critics who said he was too blond to play Bond?
A: He had no time to dye *(plus the naysayers were clearly idiots)*.

FROM ELLIOT CARVER'S
FAKE NEWS FILES ...

Live and Let Die composer George Martin was such a fan of the James Bond franchise that he named all three of his children Aston.

ALTERNATIVE TITLES FOR
TOMORROW NEVER DIES

The White Knight Rises
Last Tangle With Paris
Dude Where's My Carver?
Once Upon A Time ... with Spottiswoode
White Men Can HALO Jump

Here is the church,
And here are the people.
Don't look inside,
I nerve-gassed all the people.

LICENCE TO TRIPLE BILL

Some unorthodox Bond threesomes

The 'Megalomaniacal Villain's Monorail' Triple Bill
(Notably, two of these were directed by celebrated monorail propagandist Lewis Gilbert)
You Only Live Twice: There's unusually earthbound shuttles for the spacemen inside Blofeld's volcano base.
Live and Let Die: Drug lord diplomat Dr Kananga really is well-connected thanks to the monorail inside his subterranean San Monique HQ.
The Spy Who Loved Me: Minions on missions can trundle about Stromberg's supertanker thanks to his maritime monorail.

The 'Mongoose' Triple Bill
(Ferret out these references if you can)
Dr. No: 'Did you ever see a mongoose dance or a scorpion with sunstroke sting itself to death?' asks Honey Ryder, perhaps fresh from bingeing a Sir David Attenborough box set.

Live and Let Die: When Rosie Carver is horrified to find a dead – and somewhat barbequed – snake in her hotel bathroom, Bond retorts, 'I should have told you … never go in there without a mongoose.'

Casino Royale: Finally we see a mongoose dance and understand why one might make a formidable foe for a snake when the two creatures do battle for the benefit of Madagascar's easily amused gambling community.

The 'Horse's Arse' Triple Bill
(What, no Pegasus?)

Moonraker: Bond fires a tranquilizer dart in M's office, it hits a military portrait on the wall, squarely in the rear end of a horse.

Octopussy: Bond flies an Acrostar jet out of the prosthetic hindquarters of a stallion in a horsebox, as you do.

The Living Daylights: Kara compares Bond to the 'back end of horse' during a romantic interlude in Tangier. Who says romance is dead?

ALTERNATIVE TITLES FOR *THE WORLD IS NOT ENOUGH*

King's Ransom
Renard with a Vengeance
My Bloody Valentin
Dude, Where's My Caviar?
Cigar Girl, Interrupted

CLASSIC BOND QUOTES

James Bond: 'You don't have to be Klaus Hergesheimer to work here, but it helps.' (*Diamonds Are Forever*, 1971)

THOUGHTS FROM THE CUBBY HOLE ...

A startling majority of Bond composers have surnames that are also first names: Monty Norman, John Barry, David Arnold, George Martin and um ... Eric Sarah.

For Your Eyes Only spin-off movie proposal: *Nobody Does It Feta: Melina's Greek Tragedy.*

FROM ELLIOT CARVER'S
FAKE NEWS FILES …

The marine-life-obsessed Karl Stromberg advised with the casting for the twentieth Bond film *Die Another Day*, hence its stars Colin **Salmon**, Rosamund **Pike**, **Halibut** Berry and Dame Judi **Tench**.

SPIN-OFF MOVIE PROPOSALS

Saucy sex romp starring *The World Is Not Enough*'s lascivious MI6 physician Dr Molly Warmflash, called *No Time To Diagnose: The Doctor Warmflash Diaries*.

Poignant romantic comedy detailing how gay assassins Mr Wint and Mr Kidd got together, called *Til Death Us Do Part*.

Origin story for Goldfinger's awesome border control gun-toting granny, entitled *Nan of Steel*.

POTENTIAL *OCTOPUSSY* SEQUELS

Nonapussy
John Glen II: The Wrath of Khan
Eggpisode 2: Attack of the Clowns
The Farce Awakens
A View to a Kill

THOUGHTS FROM THE CUBBY HOLE …

If Bond is so good at checking the immediate vicinity for bugs, how come he doesn't detect the one up Saunder's arse in *The Living Daylights*?

ALTERNATIVE TITLES FOR
DIE ANOTHER DAY

Are you Havana Laugh?
Frost/Vixen
Apocalypse Zao
In Bad With Madonna
I Can't Believe It's Not Better

FROM ELLIOT CARVER'S FAKE NEWS FILES …

Octopussy's Indian scenes were shot entirely on location for authenticity. Visit any market square in India and you're totes guaranteed to encounter sword-swallowers, firewalkers and beardy gurus sleeping on beds of nails.

SHADY TREE'S DODGY DAD JOKES

Q: Did you hear about the guy who kept hallucinating blurry images of Donald Trump practicing witchcraft inside James Bond's underwater car?
A: He had an out of focus, hocus pocus, POTUS lotus psychosis.

Q: What's the difference between *Live and Let Die* and *Die Another Day*?
A: In one, Bond jumps over a crocodile; in the other, Bond totally jumps the shark.

Q: What's the difference between Janet Brown at the end of *For Your Eyes Only* and Paris Carver at the beginning of *Tomorrow Never Dies*?
A: One was playing Mrs Thatcher and the other was played by Mrs T. Hatcher.

When bathroom lighting fixtures in *The Man With The Golden Gun* slyly remind you of your hero's heritage as *The Saint*.

FOR ONE EYE ONLY

Remembering the Bondverse's best winkers …

James Bond right at the end of *Never Say Never Again* as he enjoys a clinch with Domino (Kim Basinger). Points awarded for: breaking the fourth wall. Points deducted for: being non-canon and generally reminding everybody that Kevin McClory was a thing.

James Bond inside the Rio ambulance in *Moonraker*. Undisputed champion of eyebrow manipulation, Moore really mixes it up here with some sly eye-flap contortion. I'm not sure whether he's conspiratorially winking at Doctor Goodhead or trying to distract their captor. Or maybe it's just a nervous twitch brought on by nearly falling off a cable car.

James Bond at the courtroom of M's public enquiry in *Skyfall*. Is this a reassuring wink to Mallory, or merely a marksmanship technique to help 007 hit his fire extinguisher target and create a smokescreen? For the purposes of this list and the book's word count, it's absolutely a wink.

Naomi, at Bond driving his Lotus in *The Spy Who Loved Me*. This winning winker performs the cheekiest, sultriest eyelid constriction ever committed to celluloid, and all while commanding the Big Bad's chopper.

Weird Poolside Fish Sculpture Thing at the end of *Licence to Kill*. The grittiest, darkest Bond movie ever? Maybe, but LTK's gravitas is somewhat undermined by the bizarre coda in its final moments when a massive statue winks at the audience. You are the weakest wink, goodbye.

ALTERNATIVE TITLES FOR
CASINO ROYALE

Love, Death & Reboots
The Texas Hold'Em Massacre
James Bond Episode XXI: A New Rope
Half Monk Half Hitman Begins
Dame Judi Dench Academy 5: Assignment Miami
International

The Spy Who Loved Me sequel detailing what Anya Amasova did next, called *XXXTRA* with the tagline: She's Bach for Moore.

THOUGHTS FROM THE CUBBY HOLE …

I'd rank *On Her Majesty's Secret Service* very highly, even with Willie Bognor's best efforts to make things go downhill rapidly.

SIR GODFREY TIBBETT'S TITBITS

Despite his name, *Thunderball* actor Rik Van Nutter was in fact in no way obsessed with heavy goods vehicles.

CLASSIC BOND QUOTES

May Day: 'He was the man at the Eiffel Tower! Sorry for not recognizing him sooner, but I've base jumped off tons of different landmarks in what looks like a really chic burqa this week, and all these old dudes shooting at me tend to blur into one.' (*A View to a Kill*, 1985)

A BOND VILLAIN LIMERICK

There once was an Alec Trevelyan,
Who became quite Machiavellian.
The British betrayed his dad,
Which made him really mad,
So he started a one-man rebellion.

THOUGHTS FROM THE CUBBY HOLE …

Deleted *Skyfall* scenes we really need to see: Craig and Judi's eleven-hour journey from London to the Scottish Highlands, up the A1(M) bickering about whether to listen to Radio 2 or Jazz FM and stopping off at South Mimms Services for wine gums, a shit and a cheeky game of Time Crisis 4 in the arcades.

ALTERNATIVE TITLES FOR
QUANTUM OF SOLACE

Medrano Most Horrid
A Mathis of Life and Death
The Bolivian Daylights
The Bourne Imitation
No Time for Another Way to Die

FROM ELLIOT CARVER'S
FAKE NEWS FILES …

Before he unexpectedly fell off a big red bridge in *A View to a Kill,* Nazi super-child Max Zorin was writing a sequel to Hitler's *Mein Kampf* called *Mein Shaft.*

LICENCE TO CHILL

The Best Bond Movies For Halloween

Spectre
A Boo to a Kill
Demons are Forever
Phantom of Solace
The Living Dead Daylights
No Tomb to Die (dir. Scary Fukunaga)

NOW DRAX WHAT I CALL MUSIC!

A James Bond Playlist

Dr. No – 'Beretta Best Forgotten'
From Russia With Love – 'Red's Red Wine'
Goldfinger – 'It's A Fort Knox Life'
Thunderball – 'Murder on the Dancefloor'
You Only Live Twice – 'Save Your Kissy For Me'
On Her Majesty's Secret Service – 'All I Want For Christmas Is Q'
Diamonds Are Forever – 'Laser in the Sky with Diamonds'
Live and Let Die – 'Samedi Bloody Samedi'
The Man With The Golden Gun – 'One Fight In Bangkok'
The Spy Who Loved Me – 'Wake Me Up Before You Gogol'
Moonraker – 'A Chang Is Gonna Come'
For Your Eyes Only – 'Ice Ice Bibi'
Octopussy – 'Orlov in the First Degree'
A View to a Kill – 'Zorin Seems To Be The Hardest Word'

The Living Daylights – 'I'm Just a Cellist Guy'
Licence to Kill – 'Isthmus Have Been Love But It's Over Now'
GoldenEye – 'Sweet Caroline' (evaluations never felt so good)
Tomorrow Never Dies – 'From Paris To Wai Lin'
The World Is Not Enough – 'My Funny Valentin'
Die Another Day – 'Bad'
Casino Royale – 'Careless Vesper'
Quantum of Solace – 'Strawberry Fields Forever' (hyperactive edit)
Skyfall – 'What's The Story Helen McCrory?'
Spectre – 'A Whiter Shade of Pale King'
No Time to Die – 'It's A Kind of Malek'

ALTERNATIVE TITLES FOR *SKYFALL*

The Magnificent Severine
See You Back at the Lodge
Dude, Where's Macau?
Rise of the Silva Surfer
Dial-up M for Murder

SPIN-OFF MOVIE PROPOSALS

Quantum of Solace's corrupt CIA section chief Gregg Beam stars in a globetrotting comedy of errors, called *Mr Beam's Holiday*.

Bond's 'brother from Langley' Felix spends a month clearing up the mess wrought by an extended action sequence at Miami International Airport, called *28 Days Leiter*.

Live and Let Die's main antagonist gets increasingly irate about the measly size of his teacups, entitled *Mr Big's Trouble With Little China*.

FROM ELLIOT CARVER'S
FAKE NEWS FILES

Although David Bowie turned down the role of Zorin in *A View to a Kill,* he loaned the hairpiece from his role as Jareth the Goblin King in *Labyrinth* to leading lady Tanya Roberts for the duration of filming.

ALTERNATIVE TITLES FOR *SPECTRE*

The Dropped Bollock
The Importance of Being Ernst
O Stepbrother Where Art Thou
Thomas Newman 2: You Only Write The Same Score Twice
One Flew Oberhauser's Cuckoo Nest

FROM ELLIOT CARVER'S
FAKE NEWS FILES …

Despite claims of equine mistreatment on the set of *Never Say Never Again* – where a horse was dropped into the sea from a great height – the beast in question received full rehabilitation and went on to enjoy a notable racing career, finishing just half a length behind Pegasus in the 4.20 at Ascot two years later.

SIR GODFREY TIBBETT'S TITBITS

The profound sadness often felt upon hearing Eric Serra's 'The Experience of Love' over the end credits of *GoldenEye* is known medically as post-Natalya depression.

LESS HIGHBROW, MOORE EYEBROW

What if Roger Moore had stuck around for Bond's sixteenth adventure, *Licence to Kill*?

Renowned for being (at the time of its release in 1989) the grittiest Bond movie yet thanks to Timothy Dalton's no-nonsense portrayal, here's how the script might have taken a lighter tone with some choice RogBond quips …

In the pre-title sequence, a wedding-bound Bond helps groom Felix capture drug lord Sanchez in a daring aerial manoeuvre: 'Well, it seems the Best Man really did win …'

During fisticuffs at the WaveKrest marine research facility, Bond throws an assailant into a vat full of quivering maggots: 'Try worming your way out of that one.' Later in the same scene, Bond knocks a security guard into an electric eel tank: 'I do hope there's no … eel feelings.'

🔫 Upon discovering that Felix's bride Della has been brutally murdered: 'You could say this has become a matter of ... wife and death.'

🔫 Q presents Bond with his palm-reading 'signature gun' gadget: 'Well, I dislike autograph hunters as much as the next man, Q, but don't you think that's a little extreme?'

🔫 Milton Krest's bonce explodes spectacularly in a decompression chamber while a concealed Bond looks on: 'Well, I er ... guess the pressure went to his head. Krest in peace.'

🔫 Bond skilfully drives a big-rig tanker through a petrol slick on fire and flips it onto its side to avoid an incoming stinger missile: 'I always did know how to articulate myself ...'

ALTERNATIVE TITLES FOR
NO TIME TO DIE

A Matera Life and Death
Keep Calm and Cary Fukunaga On
Daniel Craig 5: Not Quite as Fast but Still Furious
SwannSong
Safin Wicked This Way Comes

QUANTUM OF SILLINESS
WILL RETURN

in

YOU ONLY LAUGH
TWICE

YOU MIGHT ALSO BE INTERESTED IN ...

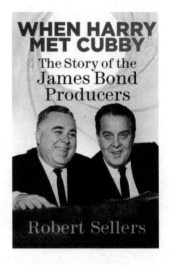

978 0 7509 9042 4